TIME
FOR KIDS

All in a Day's Work

Animator

Blanca Apodaca
Michael Serwich

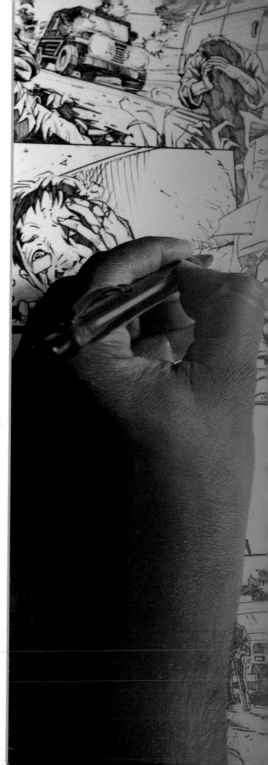

Consultants

Timothy Rasinski, Ph.D.
Kent State University

Lori Oczkus
Literacy Consultant

Paula Spence
Art Director, Cartoon Network

Based on writing from
TIME For Kids. *TIME For Kids* and the *TIME For Kids* logo are registered trademarks of TIME Inc. Used under license.

Publishing Credits

Dona Herweck Rice, *Editor-in-Chief*
Lee Aucoin, *Creative Director*
Jamey Acosta, *Senior Editor*
Courtney Patterson, *Designer*
Stephanie Reid, *Photo Editor*
Rane Anderson, *Contributing Author*
Rachelle Cracchiolo, *M.S.Ed., Publisher*

Image Credits: pp.17 (bottom right), 24, 24–25, 28 (right), 34–35, 45, 61, Alamy; p.25 (bottom) Associated Press; p.16 (bottom left) Bridgeman Art Library; pp.20–21, 33, 37–38 Corbis; p.51 Vancouver Film School/Flickr; pp.7–8, 10–11, 16 (top right), 18–19, 28 (left), 28–31, 42, 52–53, 63 Getty Images; pp.12, 17 LOC [LC-DIG-ppmsc-02839]; p.17 (top left), 30, 47 (bottom) Newscom; p.14 ccostas@sacbee.com/Newscom; pp.2–3, 21 (bottom), 44–45 EPA/Newscom; p.46 ITAR-TASS/Newscom; pp.18, 35 KRT/Newscom; p.49 Lucas Film/20th Century Fox/Album/Newscom; p.57 MCT/Newscom; pp.32–33, 54–55 REUTERS/Newscom; p.20 Nate Beckett/Splash News/Newscom; pp.45–46 ZUMA Press/Newscom; pp.9, 15–16, 26–27, 32–33, 40–41, 43 (illustrations) Timothy J. Bradley; pp.6, 13 Public domain, via Wikimedia Commons; All other images from Shutterstock.

Teacher Created Materials

5301 Oceanus Drive
Huntington Beach, CA 92649-1030
http://www.tcmpub.com

ISBN 978-1-4333-4907-2
© 2013 Teacher Created Materials, Inc.
Printed in China
Nordica.082019.CA21901097

TABLE OF CONTENTS

ART HISTORY

It is said that a picture is worth a thousand words. But what does that mean? Pictures tell stories about the past, present, and future. They tell stories about life. Our fascination with art stretches back in time to the first cave paintings of animals.

Today, we use more than a single picture on a cave wall to tell a story. Animated stories are made up of thousands of images. Instead of one still image, artists draw many images. A series of pictures may show someone holding a bow, shooting an arrow, and watching it fly across the forest to wound a monster. Some moving pictures are made up of pictures taken with a camera. Animators can also draw or paint stories by hand or with a computer. Simple lines and colors bring characters to life. Telling stories with images is an ancient art form that continues to delight audiences around the world.

"DRAWING IS STILL BASICALLY THE SAME AS IT HAS BEEN SINCE PREHISTORIC TIMES. IT BRINGS TOGETHER MAN AND THE WORLD. IT LIVES THROUGH MAGIC."

—KEITH HARING, ARTIST

THINK LINK

- How do animators tell stories with moving pictures?
- What skills do animators need to be successful?
- Why would you like to be an animator?

SPINNING A STORY

Many creative people and their clever inventions led to the movie magic we enjoy today. The **zoetrope** (ZOH-ee-trohp) came before the spread of electricity. Invented in the 1880s, it was one of the first machines to make moving pictures. The zoetrope contained a strip of pictures in a cylinder. Each picture was slightly different from the one next to it. Small windows lined the cylinder. The viewer spun the zoetrope and looked through the windows. With a twist of the wrist, the images seemed to come to life. The zoetrope was one of the first ways to present a short story that could be watched again and again.

One of the first zoetropes was made in China almost 2,000 years ago. It was called a *chao hua chich kuan*. The phrase can be translated as "the pipe which makes fantasies appear."

Inside a Zoetrope

A panel of drawings shows a character's slightly changing position in each image.

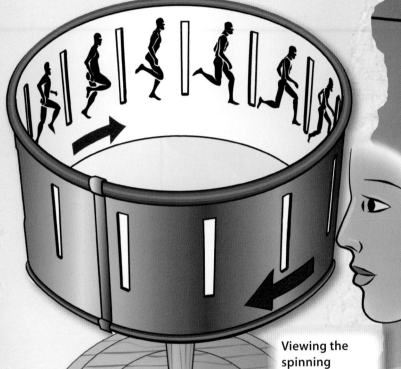

Viewing the spinning images through slits creates the illusion of movement.

The cylinder spins on a stand.

FLIPPING OUT

The first **flip-book** was **patented** in 1868. The concept was similar to a zoetrope, but smaller. Flip-books are made up of a series of pictures. Each picture in the book is drawn on a separate piece of paper. The idea is to draw each picture slightly differently from the one before. The drawings are then stacked in order and flipped through quickly. As they flip, the images appear to move.

Your Mind's Eye

If you close your eyes after staring at a candle flame, you will still "see" it in your mind. This is known as *persistence of vision*. This same illusion makes the images in a flip-book appear to be moving.

The filoscope is an early example of a flip-book.

Make Your Own

Anyone can make a flip-book. All it takes is paper, something to write with, and a good imagination!

1. Draw a simple character in 10 slightly different positions.

2. Cut out the images.

3. Organize them in order from top to bottom.

4. Staple the book together on the left side.

5. Flip through the book using your right thumb.

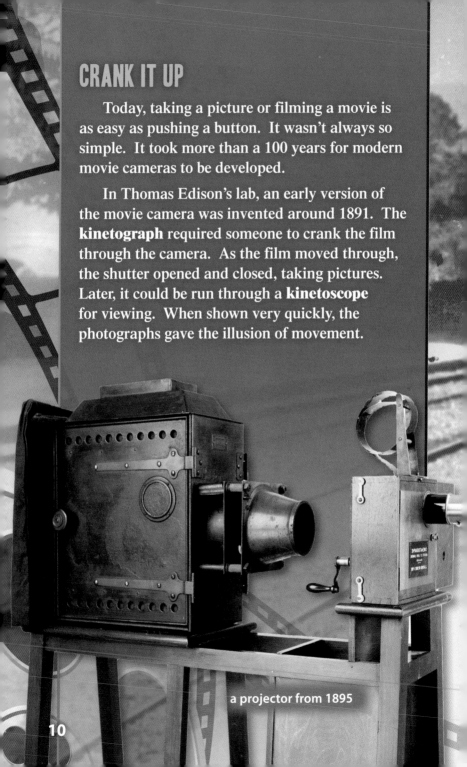

CRANK IT UP

Today, taking a picture or filming a movie is as easy as pushing a button. It wasn't always so simple. It took more than a 100 years for modern movie cameras to be developed.

In Thomas Edison's lab, an early version of the movie camera was invented around 1891. The **kinetograph** required someone to crank the film through the camera. As the film moved through, the shutter opened and closed, taking pictures. Later, it could be run through a **kinetoscope** for viewing. When shown very quickly, the photographs gave the illusion of movement.

a projector from 1895

> "I THINK CINEMA, MOVIES, AND MAGIC HAVE ALWAYS BEEN CLOSELY ASSOCIATED. THE VERY EARLIEST PEOPLE WHO MADE FILM WERE MAGICIANS."
>
> —FRANCIS FORD COPPOLA, DIRECTOR

Run!

Arrival of a Train at La Ciotat was a short film made by the Lumière brothers in 1895. It showed a train pulling into a station. When people first saw the movie, some thought the train was headed right for them. Scared, some people in the front rows panicked and ran out of the movie theater!

INTO THE PROJECTOR

Winsor McCay was a comic strip artist in the 1900s. He wanted to combine his art style with animation. One year and 10,000 sheets of paper later, McCay had a ten-minute film.

Just as in flip-books, each image was drawn to look a little different than the one before. But after each drawing was complete, it was photographed. Then, the photograph was developed. Finally, it was run through a movie projector onto a screen. This was the first time anyone had tried this. The movie thrilled audiences. It was one of the first steps toward modern animation.

Meet Gertie

The most famous of McCay's animated characters was a bashful dinosaur named Gertie. When the short film was finished, McCay projected his film, *Gertie the Dinosaur*, for an audience. Some of the audience members searched behind the screen for wires that controlled the dinosaur. They couldn't believe their eyes!

Gertie the Dinosaur

VINSOR McCAY'S "GERTIE"
WONDERFULLY TRAINED DINOSAURUS

WINSOR McCAY
AMERICA'S GREATEST
CARTOONIST.

A Prehistoric Animal
that Lived Thirteen Mil-
lion Years Ago, Brought
Back to Life. A Most
Marvellous Work of Art,
Science and Humor.
She's a Scream

A Star Is Born

Gertie was the first main character created specifically
for movies. Before then, artists had mostly used
characters found in newspaper comic strips.

X OFFICE
FEATURE
FILM

Released through **BOX OFFICE ATTRACTION CO.**

13

WILLIAM FOX PRESIDENT   EXCHANGES IN ALL PRINCIPAL CITIES.

EASY DOES IT

McCay was forced to take a break from animation for many years. When he returned to the art form, he was one of the first to create movies using **cel** animation. A cel is a clear sheet of **cellulose acetate**. The animator draws a cartoon on a top sheet. Because it is clear, it can be set on top of another cel. The first cel may show a character. The second cel may show the **background**. Both layers are then photographed together. This forms a single **frame** in a film. Using this technique saved time. Animators didn't have to spend weeks redrawing backgrounds or other small elements.

an animator holding up a cel

Early Mickey Mouse cartoons and episodes of *The Simpsons* also used cel animation.

Cartoons Get Real

In early cartoons, it was hard to make characters move like humans. Animator Max Fleischer solved this problem in the early 1900s when he invented the **rotoscope**. The term *rotoscoping* is still used to describe a modern computer process. In this process, live-action footage is covered over with **digital** animation.

glass plate

projector

rotoscope

The rotoscope projects live-action images, one frame at a time, onto the back of a frosted glass plate.

The cel is placed on top of the glass. The artist traces the live-action images. The result is characters that move just like humans.

The History of Animation

Ever since the first artist tried to animate moving pictures, animation has always been about more than turning simple lines into stories that move.

1834

1868

The zoetrope is invented by British mathematician William George Horner.

The flip-book is patented by John Barnes Linnett.

1914

1917

The process for cel animation is developed by Earl Hurd and J.R. Bray.

The rotoscope is patented by Max Fleischer.

Today, animation from Europe and Japan is taking the world by storm.

1889

The kinetoscope is invented in Thomas Edison's lab using celluloid strip film.

1911

Winsor McCay creates one of the first animated sequences.

1951

Color television is introduced in the United States.

1995

Toy Story, the first fully computer-generated 3D-feature film, is released.

MOVING PICTURES

Zap! Pow! Boing! Millions of kids wake up early on Saturdays to watch cartoons. These shows may seem like a quick treat, but even today, a lot of work goes into creating these mini masterpieces. It takes a team of artists to make just one minute of action. A show that lasts for 30 minutes may take months to create. It may even take years!

Just like any team, every member has a different talent. Some members are artists who draw pictures. Others are writers. Some prefer to work digitally. Others use pen and paper. What's important is that they work together to make audiences smile.

A character for the show *King of the Hill* is sketched by an animator.

"ANIMATION MEANS NOT ONLY TO SET THINGS IN MOTION, BUT ALSO, MORE PROFOUNDLY, TO BRING THEM TO LIFE."
—A.O. SCOTT, FILM CRITIC

ONCE UPON A TIME

Every cartoon begins as an idea. The writers gather together. They talk about the stories they might tell in a new TV show. They decide on a **premise** for the first episode. The premise explains the story in just a few short sentences. This will help them sell the idea to the key people at the studio. The **producer** must approve the premise for the new cartoon.

After the writers have approval, the story must be expanded. The writers might write an outline first, adding details as they go along. Then, they write the story as a **script**.

Drawing from Life

Writers draw inspiration from their lives to create characters and stories. Matt Groening, the creator of *The Simpsons*, named Homer, Marge, Lisa, and Maggie Simpson after his parents and sisters.

Planning takes more time in the beginning, but it's an important part of the creative process. Planning and reviewing their work helps artists create a final product they are happy with.

Animators discuss a new idea.

CHARACTER DEVELOPMENT

As they create the script, writers must think about the characters and setting. The story needs an introduction, problem, solution, and conclusion. The writers also pay attention to **voice.** The voice doesn't just come from the way the characters talk. It's how the story is told. Word choice, the pacing of events, and each character's personality all make up the voice of the script.

Where Am I?

When considering the setting, there is so much more to consider than just the place. Writers take into account the time period, including technology, or inventions, of that era. They also think about the weather. A sunny day works well with a cheerful scene. Dark clouds or a night sky may fit better with an angry scene.

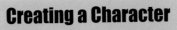

Creating a Character

To develop a new character, writers think about the following elements: name, secret identity, occupation, super powers, weaknesses, history, living or dead relatives, goal or purpose in life, and appearance.

STORYBOARDING

Once the script is written, **storyboard** artists decide what parts of the story are most important. Storyboarding takes the story from written words and turns it into pictures. The artists draw small pictures to show what happens at each point in the story. Then, the pictures are lined up on a large board. This is an easy way for the team to see if the story makes sense.

In the 1920s, "story sketches" were used to plan *Steamboat Willie*, the first official Mickey Mouse short film.

Inventing Stories

It's common to use storyboards today. But when animators started using them in the 1930s, it was a huge step. It saved time and helped them plan out each scene. Webb Smith was the first to use storyboards to make cartoons.

Disney artists were some of the first to use storyboards.

What's Your Vision?

Storyboard artists have a lot to think about. What type of facial expression matches a character's dialogue? Should the picture show a close-up of the character's face? What colors should be used in the background? Follow the steps below to create your own storyboard.

1 Fold a piece of paper into halves until you have eight boxes to use as frames. Draw lines for making notes to the director.

2 Choose a scene from your favorite book and turn it into a short script.

3 Draw pictures of the important parts.

4 Consider the best way to convey your idea to the audience. For example, how will you show that your character is happy or sad?

5 Use single frames to highlight a gesture or show a close-up.

6 Review your storyboard to see how it might transfer to animation. Is there anything you could add or take away?

VOICE TALENT

Production is under way. Artists have imagined how the film will look. Now, it's time to add sound. Sound helps simple line drawings come alive. The characters' voices are performed by actors. Their voices are recorded by **sound engineers**. **Music producers** oversee work in a recording studio. The actors who perform the voices are chosen carefully to match each part.

The actors practice reading the script. They find the best way to say their lines. A simple change can make a line feel more moving. Finally, they go into the studio and record their lines.

What's Up, Doc?

Even if you have never heard of Mel Blanc, you have probably heard his voice. For decades, he was the voice for dozens of Warner Brothers cartoon characters. Bugs Bunny, Daffy Duck, Tweety Bird, and Pepe Le Pew are just a few. His vocal talents and comic timing earned him the title The Man of a Thousand Voices.

Because animated stories can take place in strange and amazing places, actors can sometimes find themselves reading lines they wouldn't say anywhere else.

Special microphones record the actors' voices. Later, the shape of the characters' mouths will be matched to the sound. Sometimes, the actors sing. **Composers** write the songs. Much like writing and drawing, the composing, acting, and recording can be hard work. But sound can make each scene more fun to watch.

Actor Robert DeNiro records his lines for the animated movie *Shark Tale*.

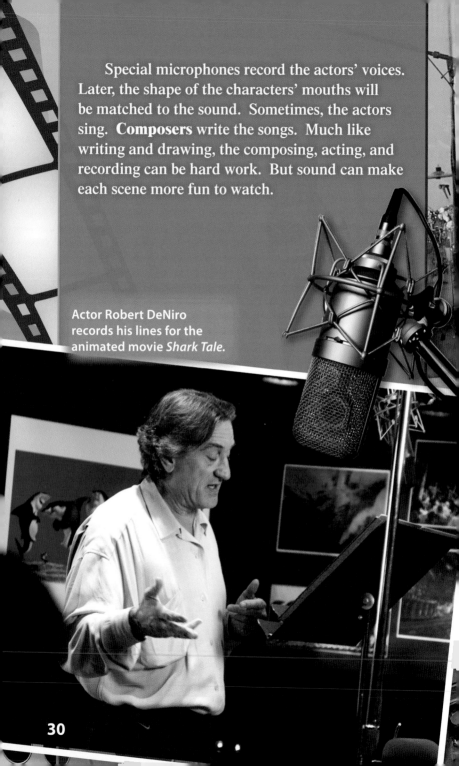

Rockin' Tunes

Cartoon Network has a recording studio right next to its art studios. Artists, actors, producers, and musicians work side by side to create terrific artwork and soundtracks for cartoons.

Music Notes

Theme songs start cartoons off on a fun note. The right song can set the tone for the entire show. And the catchiest tunes are hard to forget!

MAKING A MOUTH MOVE

When we talk, our mouths take on different shapes. Each shape corresponds to a different sound. For example, when someone says the *o* sound in the word *boat*, the mouth forms a round *o* shape. The *b* and the *t* sounds in *boat* form other mouth shapes. Each specific sound is a **phoneme**.

Animators use phonemes to make characters look like people when they talk. They draw pictures of each character's mouth making the different sounds. When they are filmed and played back quickly, they look like mouths talking.

Phoneme Mouth Chart

/ă/ as in *mat*   /ēē/ as in *cheese*

/m/ as in *milk*

Experiment

Watch an animated film. Repeat what the character says while you look in the mirror. Watch your mouth carefully. Now compare it with the character's mouth. Did the animators do their job? Did your mouth shape match the character's?

/k/ as in *cow*

/o/ as in *no*

/w/ as in *water*

Stop-Motion

Stop-motion is a type of animation. It is used around the world. And like any animation, it requires patience. Artists build figures that look like dolls or puppets. They move the figures a little bit at a time. A picture is taken before they are moved again. Later, when the pictures are quickly shown in order, the figures appear to come to life. Stop-motion can be made with clay figures, as in the *Wallace and Gromit* films. It can also be made with moveable parts, as in *Fantastic Mr. Fox*.

Director Wes Anderson adjusts a character's costume on the set of *Fantastic Mr. Fox.*

Claymation

Animation created with clay objects using the stop-motion technique is called *claymation*. Animators must position and photograph a figure 24 times to get 1 second of film!

When animators use stop-motion, they create multiple versions of each character's head. They move the faces to form different expressions and phonemes.

CREATING A WORLD

The area behind the main characters is the background. It sets the mood and tells you where the story is taking place. Artists draw the scenery in a wide variety of styles. They choose colors and shapes that will help tell the story in ways the audience might not notice right away.

Props are objects like toys, chairs, bikes, and other things the character may use in a scene. Prop and background artists spend their days drawing and painting pictures with paper, pencils, paints, and computers. The scenery and props are later layered digitally around the characters.

Field Work

When animators need inspiration, they turn to real life. they need to study animals, they go to a zoo. They ight even go on safari in Africa. That's what some nimators did before working on *The Lion King*. They udied the movements and habits of lions and other ldlife. Their research gave them the inspiration they eeded to tell an amazing story.

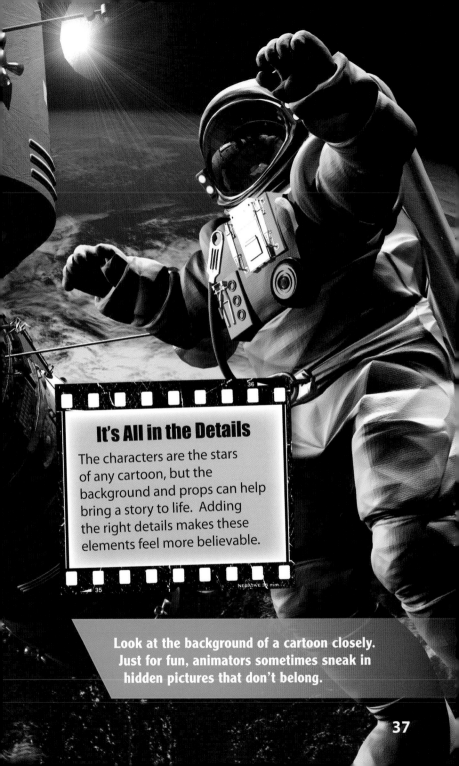

It's All in the Details

The characters are the stars of any cartoon, but the background and props can help bring a story to life. Adding the right details makes these elements feel more believable.

Look at the background of a cartoon closely. Just for fun, animators sometimes sneak in hidden pictures that don't belong.

ANIMATICS

An **animatic** is a kind of moving storyboard. A series of sketches are matched with a rough soundtrack. This helps animators see how all the final elements will work together. It can be difficult to know how the piece will look when it's finished. The animatics help them spot any problems. If the story is being told too quickly or too slowly, they can fix it before the final animation is complete. Animators use animatics to check their progress throughout production.

That's Toontastic!

Today, it's easier than ever to become an animator. Software and apps give artists all the tools they need to tell a story. The Toontastic app lets kids animate pictures and add music to tell original stories. You can even animate your own artwork!

Some DVDs come with the original animatics so you can watch and compare them to the final animation.

DIG DEEPER!

Making It Look Natural

Frank Thomas and Ollie Johnston were two of the original great animators at Walt Disney Studios in the 1930s. They created a list of principles of animation that make drawings of motion appear more real. Here are a few of their guidelines.

Squashing and stretching gives weight and volume to an object or character as it moves.

Anticipation is movement that helps the audience know what action is coming. Think of a pitcher's windup or a golfer's backswing.

Follow through occurs when a character stops moving, but smaller parts such as hair, clothes, or floppy ears keep moving.

Secondary action is additional action that supports the main movement as it happens. As a character's body moves, smaller parts also move. Arms swing, a horse's hair bounces, or perhaps a skirt flows.

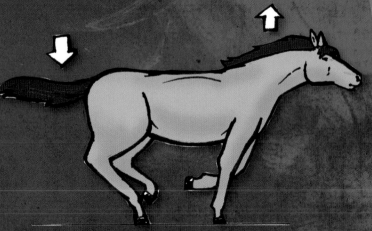

X MARKS THE SPOT

The animation director looks over the story, the characters, the props, the backgrounds, and the animatics. It's a big job, and it's important to get it right. Now, it is time to prepare the exposure sheet, or **X-sheet**. The X-sheet tells how to draw each action in the story. It shows how and when to draw mouth shapes to match the recorded words. Most importantly, it tells what happens during each moment of the cartoon.

After the X-sheet is prepared, it is sent to the next group of animators. They begin to draw the entire cartoon, **frame** by frame. Each frame changes slightly from the frame before it. When these still pictures are lined up and shot on film, they will be animated.

Drawing from Experience

Not all animators go to art school. Many learn by copying the works of others. John Kricfalusi, the creator of *Ren & Stimpy*, is a self-taught artist. He trained himself as a boy by copying drawings from newspapers and comic books.

X-Sheet Breakdown

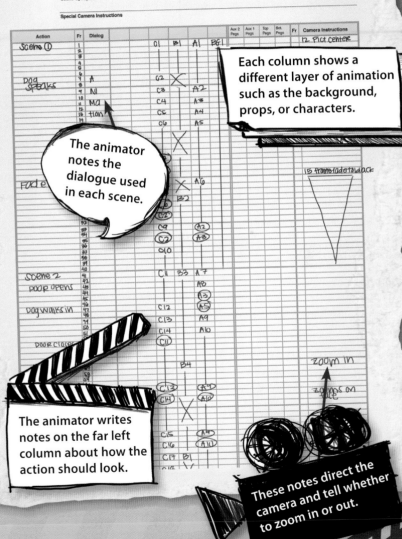

Each column shows a different layer of animation such as the background, props, or characters.

The animator notes the dialogue used in each scene.

The animator writes notes on the far left column about how the action should look.

These notes direct the camera and tell whether to zoom in or out.

Project Management

Every animation project requires careful planning. The director must know how long each project will take and plan time with the team accordingly. Every member of the team needs to understand his or her job and when it's due. Check out the production schedule below.

Key
Dark Blue=pre-production
Light Blue=production
Purple=post-production

Month	January	February	March	April	May	June	July	August	September	
Storyboarding	dark blue	dark blue	dark blue	dark blue	dark blue	dark blue				
Animatics						light blue	light blue	light blue	light blue	
Animation						light blue	light blue	light blue	light blue	
Sound Effects						purple	purple	purple	purple	
Test Screening						purple				

From pen to silver screen, *Snow White and the Seven Dwarfs* took three years to make.

**STOP!
THINK...**

- How many months will it take to complete this project?

- Why do some parts of the project take longer than others?

- Which step looks the most important?

October	November	December	January	February	March	April	May	June	July	August	September	October	November	December

POST-PRODUCTION

Post-production happens after all the writing and drawing has come to an end. **Editors** review the animation. They make corrections. The **art director** watches the cartoon to see if it matches the original vision for the film. The cartoon looks almost finished. But it will be checked for any last-minute problems. The animated action can be watched without sound. After the mistakes are fixed and changes are made, sound layers can be added.

The Jazz Singer

This was the first "talkie" picture, which meant people could finally hear the actors talking in a movie.

A scene from *Masha and the Bear* is finished digitally.

ep04a_11_f_136_cam
Focal Length: 75

frame 11 / 13
timecode 00:1

30 40 50 60 70

Walt Disney with an early version of Mickey Mouse

36

A Disney Idea!

Walt Disney and Ub Iwerks saw *The Jazz Singer* and decided to try adding sound to their own cartoon. Their film *Steamboat Willie* starred Mickey Mouse.

35 NEGATIVE 35 mm

THE MIX

A cartoon without sound just isn't as fun. Music and **sound effects** are mixed together to create the complete soundtrack. Music is composed and then recorded. Sound effects such as doors slamming, feet stomping, and phones ringing are also recorded in the studio. The mix builds tension. It helps the audience know when to feel scared or happy, nervous or relieved. All these sound effects take a lot of thought. But music and sounds make cartoons come to life.

Music Makes a Difference

Music can help the viewer understand the mood of the scene. If something sad is happening, the director may add slow music to a movie. If the characters are happy, the music may be more upbeat and cheerful. Music can convey anger if it's loud and booming, or suspense if it's slow and lingering.

Just like the *Star Wars* character Darth Vader, many cartoon characters have a musical signature that lets viewers know when they are about to enter a scene.

Leitmotifs

A musical phrase or melody that plays when a certain character appears is called a *leitmotif* (LAHYT-moh-teef). Probably the best example is the two notes that play in *Jaws* whenever a shark is near. In *Star Wars*, Darth Vader also has his own leitmotif called *The Imperial Theme*. The cackling wicked witch from *The Wizard of Oz* shared her leitmotif with the mean Miss Gulch, connecting the two characters.

DIG DEEPER!

Noise Makers

In a cartoon, most sounds need to be made from scratch. The people who make the sound effects for cartoons are **foley artists.** They make these sounds with anything that can make noise. The foley artists then record these noises while watching the cartoon so that the sounds and images match perfectly.

A foley artist drops pennies onto a drum to create the sound of rain falling on a tin roof.

Coconut halves become horse hooves when slapped against different surfaces.

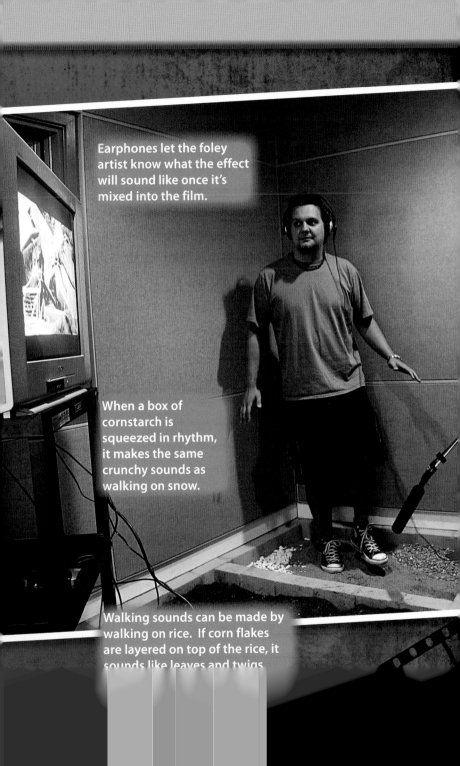

Earphones let the foley artist know what the effect will sound like once it's mixed into the film.

When a box of cornstarch is squeezed in rhythm, it makes the same crunchy sounds as walking on snow.

Walking sounds can be made by walking on rice. If corn flakes are layered on top of the rice, it sounds like leaves and twigs.

TESTING, TESTING, ONE, TWO, THREE

Before the film is shown to a large audience, it is shown to a small group of people. Writers and directors watch as the test audience views the film. They want to see which jokes get the loudest laughs. They look to see if the audience is bored during certain parts. At the end, they may ask the audience questions. They want to know if any parts were confusing. The creators of the animation want the audience to love it. This is their last chance to make any changes. Soon, their work can be enjoyed by millions of people around the world.

a test audience

Something Is in the Air...

When a cartoon *airs*, that means it is finally shown on TV. Some animators don't see the final cut of their cartoon until the day it airs. They watch it for the first time with the rest of the world.

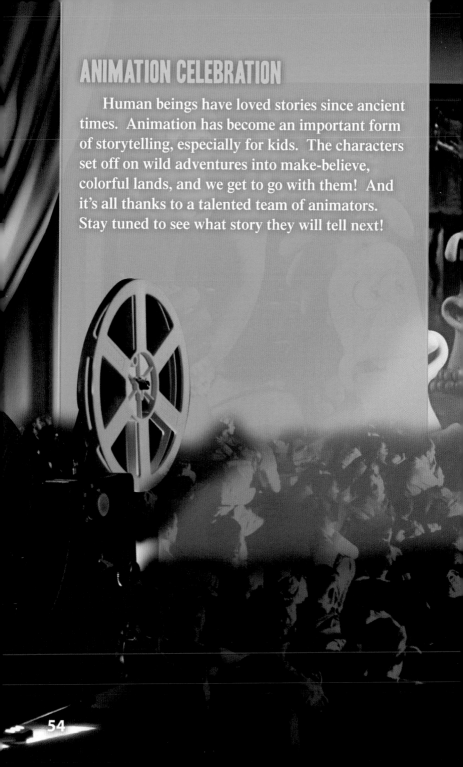

ANIMATION CELEBRATION

Human beings have loved stories since ancient times. Animation has become an important form of storytelling, especially for kids. The characters set off on wild adventures into make-believe, colorful lands, and we get to go with them! And it's all thanks to a talented team of animators. Stay tuned to see what story they will tell next!

a clip from the movie
Chicken Run

Meet an Animator

Meet art director Paula Spence from Cartoon Network, a TV station that airs mostly cartoons 24 hours a day, 365 days a year. She sat down with writers Blanca Apodaca and Michael Serwich to talk about why she loves her job so much.

Michael: Hi Paula! Thanks for giving us a tour of Cartoon Network. What part do you play in making cartoons?

Paula: I oversee the designers and painters who draw and color the backgrounds, characters, and props in cartoons. I teach new artists to match the style of the show. And I make sure we draw and paint everything we need to make a complete cartoon.

Blanca: What did you do to prepare yourself for a career in animation?

Paula: I took a lot of art classes in high school and college. I have a degree in **illustration**, so I can draw anything real or imagined. Also, I have practiced with many different styles, which is helpful in moving from show to show because animators need to be flexible and creative. Organization skills help, too, especially in managing all the artists on one show and making sure everything gets done.

Michael: What do you love the best about your job?

Paula: I love working with all of the artists and writers. Everyone is creative and unique, so every day is a new adventure.

GLOSSARY

animatic—a series of still images shown with dialogue or music that gives a rough view of how an animated project will look and feel once completed

art director—a person who works with other artists to produce the overall look and feel of a film

background—the part of a scene that is furthest away from the viewer

cel—a transparent sheet that animators draw on

cellulose acetate—a material film is made of

composers—people who write music professionally

digital—electronic and computerized technology

editors—people who add or subtract elements from a film or video to help improve a story

flip-book—pieces of paper with images drawn on them that, when flipped through, create the illusion of motion

foley artists—people who make sound effects for cartoons

frame—one of the drawings in a comic strip

illustration—drawings of images or characters

kinetograph—an early device used to record motion

kinetoscope—a device that displays a series of pictures moving quickly to create the illusion of motion

music producers—people who oversee work in a recording studio

patented—the exclusive right to make, use, or sell an invention for a certain number of years

phoneme—distinct sounds made in speech

premise—a brief explanation which introduces a story or idea

producer—a person who oversees all aspects of production including creative, financial, and technical elements

production—the act or process of drawing and filming a new project

props—objects in a story that are not furniture or costumes

rotoscope—a piece of equipment that allows animators to project live-action images one frame at a time onto the back of frosted glass

script—a written plan for a show

sound effects—any sound, other than music or speech, used to create an effect in a film

sound engineers—people who oversee the recording of sounds or music

storyboard—a series of drawings pasted on a board that shows how the action will progress in an animated film

voice—the way a story is told through word choice, the pacing of events, and each character's personality

X-sheet—a form that describes and directs all the action, dialogue, sound, and camera work in an animation

zoetrope—a cylinder that gives the illusion of images being animated when spun

INDEX

BIBLIOGRAPHY

Cohn, Jessica. *Animator*. Gareth Stevens Publishing, 2009.

Learn how animators create the movies, video games, and cartoons that you enjoy watching and playing. Find out what they earn and how they train for this creative career.

Gray, Milton. *Cartoon Animation: Introduction to a Career*. Lion's Den Publication, 1991.

Find out more about a career in animation. You will learn what supplies are needed, how to draw and animate, plus expert tips from top animators.

Lenburg, Jeff and Chris Bailey. *The Encyclopedia of Animated Cartoons*. Checkmark Books, 2008.

This is the ultimate guide to cartoons. Learn about all the jobs involved in creating a cartoon from start to finish. You will also learn a brief history of American animation and find a reference guide mentioning every cartoon character ever created!

Priebe, Ken A. *The Art of Stop-Motion Animation*. Course Technology, 2006.

Stop-motion animation is an art form people love to watch. In this book, you will learn the history of stop-motion animation and how to create your own.

MORE TO EXPLORE

The Origins of American Animation

http://memory.loc.gov/ammem/oahtml/oahome.html

Learn about different types of early American animation, from clay and puppet animation to cut-out and pen animation.

Pixar Animation Studio

http://www.pixar.com/behind_the_scenes

Find out how a masterpiece is made. Here you will learn about the stages Pixar films go through before you see the final film.

ABCya

http://www.abcya.com/animate.htm

Create your own animated cartoon. Learn the basics of computer animation while creating your own cartoon that you can save and show your friends and family. You can start off simple, animating a bouncing ball or recreating a scene from your favorite book.

On the Move

http://www.nga.gov/kids/stella/activityflip.htm

Here you will find all you need to know to make your own flip-book. You will also learn tips and tricks to take your flip-book to the next level of animation using your computer.

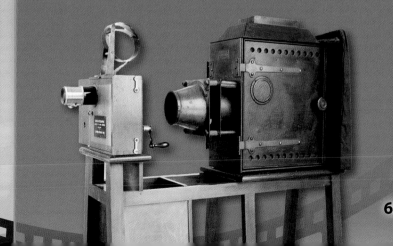

ABOUT THE AUTHORS

Michael Serwich is a professional puppeteer and performer. He has a bachelor of fine arts in playwriting from De Paul University. He writes and hosts puppet shows at The Natural History Museum of Los Angeles. His favorite puppet there is a life-size juvenile T. Rex named Hunter.

Blanca Apodaca illustrates books, and creates art for children and adults. She is the author and illustrator of *Smally's Secret Alphabook*. She also composed and performed music for two records.

Together, Blanca and her husband, Michael, write stories and build puppet shows, but their greatest creation will always be their daughter, Melody.

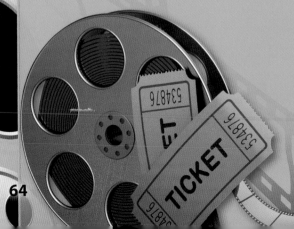